FACT AND FICTION OF AMERICAN HISTORY

FACT AND FICTION OF THE SPACE AGE

BY DOUGLAS HUSTAD

CONTENT CONSULTANT
Yanek Mieczkowski, PhD
Presidential Historian

Core Library

An Imprint of Abdo Publishing
abdobooks.com

Cover image: Astronaut Eugene A. Cernan was commander of the Apollo 17 moon mission in 1972.

abdobooks.com

Published by Abdo Publishing, a division of ABDO, PO Box 398166, Minneapolis, Minnesota 55439.

Printed in the United States of America, North Mankato, Minnesota
052021
092021

THIS BOOK CONTAINS RECYCLED MATERIALS

Cover Photo: JSC/NASA
Interior Photos: Sovfoto/Universal Images Group/Getty Images, 4–5; Bettmann/Getty Images, 8; MSFC/NASA, 10–11; Red Line Editorial, 13, 40; JSC/NASA, 17, 43; Bob Nye/LRC/NASA, 20–21, 45; GRC/NASA, 22; LRC/NASA, 25; NASA/AP Images, 27; KSC/NASA, 28–29; Shutterstock Images, 34–35; NASA, 37

Editor: Aubrey Zalewski
Series Designer: Ryan Gale

Library of Congress Control Number: 2020948270

Publisher's Cataloging-in-Publication Data

Names: Hustad, Douglas, author.
Title: Fact and fiction of the space age / by Douglas Hustad
Description: Minneapolis, Minnesota : Abdo Publishing, 2022 | Series: Fact and fiction of American history | Includes online resources and index.
Identifiers: ISBN 9781532195129 (lib. bdg.) | ISBN 9781098215439 (ebook)
Subjects: LCSH: Astronautics and civilization--Juvenile literature. | Outer space--Exploration--Juvenile literature. | Truthfulness and falsehood--Juvenile literature. | Public opinion--Juvenile literature.
Classification: DDC 973.9--dc23

CONTENTS

CHAPTER ONE

A THREAT FROM ABOVE?

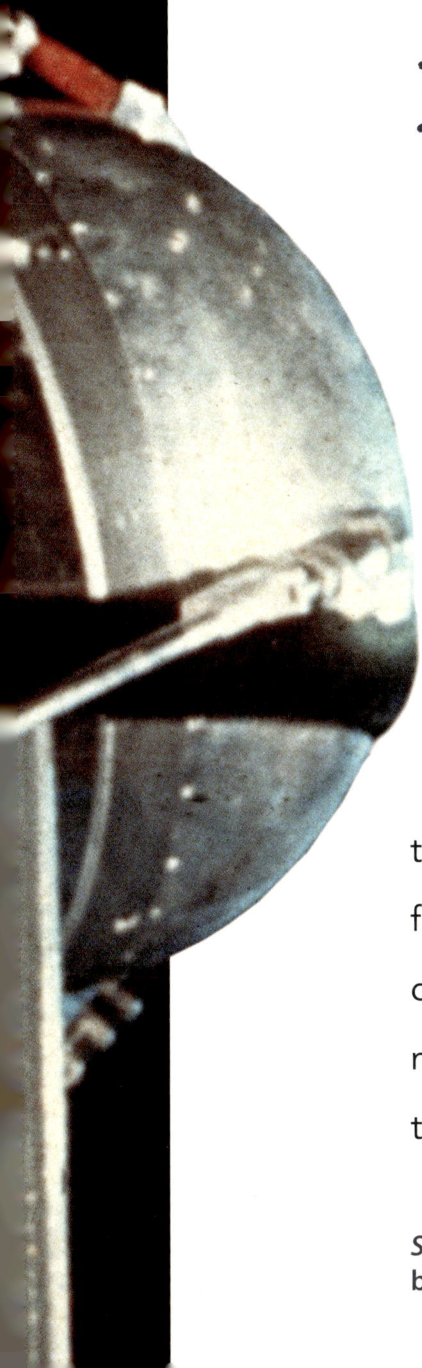

The space age began with a beep on October 4, 1957. The beep came from a tiny satellite called *Sputnik 1*. It was the first satellite made by people to orbit Earth.

But the United States didn't put it in space. The Soviet Union did. The United States and the Soviet Union both wanted to get to space. Whichever country got there first would attract global attention. The two countries were in a struggle to be the world's most powerful nation. This struggle was called the Cold War (1947–1991). The countries

***Sputnik 1* was approximately the size of a beach ball.**

THE COLD WAR

The United States and the Soviet Union were the two most powerful countries in the world after World War II (1939–1945). The Soviet Union was communist. The United States was capitalist. In communism, one party controls the country and its economy. In capitalism, the government plays a small role in the economy. Both countries wanted their way of government to become dominant in the world. The Cold War was the countries' fight for dominance. Americans constantly feared that the Cold War would break out into nuclear war.

never fought each other directly. Instead, they competed in other ways to gain power and influence. Space exploration was one of these ways. The competition became known as the space race.

Cold War fears made Americans wonder about the strange beeping object in the sky. Some worried that the United States was behind the Soviet Union in science and technology. American media outlets made a big deal about the satellite. They tried to stir up fear.

The reality was that all *Sputnik 1* could do was beep. It was no threat to anyone. But its presence showed that the Soviets could launch things into space. One day, they could launch a weapon. This unnerved some Americans. US president Dwight D. Eisenhower assured the public that *Sputnik 1* was no threat. But behind closed doors, he knew what *Sputnik 1* meant. The United States had been beaten to space. Now Americans had to respond.

THE SPACE RACE TAKES OFF

The Soviet Union and the United States battled to be first in space achievements. The Soviet Union scored many

PERSPECTIVES

SOVIET NEWSPAPERS

The Soviet Union boasted about its achievement in its newspapers. On October 5, 1957, an article in the Russian newspaper *Pravda* said:

> ***The successful launching of the first man-made Earth satellite . . . is of tremendous importance for learning the properties of cosmic space and for studying the Earth as a planet of our solar system.***

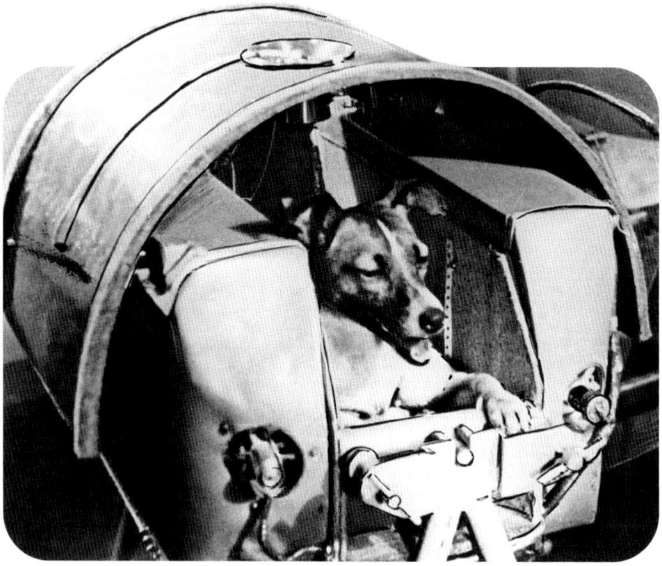

Laika the dog was the first living creature to orbit Earth.

early victories. In November 1957, it launched *Sputnik 2*. This time a dog was on board. The United States was falling behind. In 1960, John F. Kennedy was elected president. He took the space race to new heights. But it all started with *Sputnik 1*.

SEPARATING FACT FROM FICTION

American media's response to *Sputnik 1* created some of the first misconceptions of the space age. Decades later, there have been many moments of misunderstanding. But understanding the true facts of the space age allows people to see the space age's achievements as they really are.

STRAIGHT TO THE **SOURCE**

American media expressed its concerns about the *Sputnik 1* launch. Robert Hotz was editor in chief for *Aviation Weekly*. Hotz wrote on October 14, 1957:

> *We believe that the people of this country have a right to know the facts about the relative positions of the US and the Soviet Union in this technological race. . . . They have the right to find out why a nation with our vastly superior scientific, economic, and military potential is being at the very least equaled and perhaps surpassed by a country that less than two decades ago couldn't even play in the same scientific ball park. They also have the right to make decisions as to whether they want their government to maintain our current leadership of the free world regardless of the cost in dollars and sweat. . . . They are not decisions to be made arbitrarily by a [close group] of leaders in an ivory tower or on a golf course.*

Source: "One Small Ball in the Air." *NASA's Origins and the Dawn of the Space Age*, n.d., history.nasa.gov. Accessed 27 May 2020.

WHAT'S THE BIG IDEA?

Read this passage carefully. What is the main idea? Which details does Hotz use to support the main idea? Explain how two or three of those details support Hotz's point.

CHAPTER TWO

PROJECT APOLLO

President Kennedy made a famous speech on May 25, 1961. He announced an ambitious goal. By the end of the 1960s, the United States would land men on the moon.

On July 20, 1969, Neil Armstrong and Buzz Aldrin fulfilled that goal. The astronauts took the first steps on the moon's surface during the Apollo 11 mission. Ten more men went back in five more missions. The moon landing is now remembered as one of the greatest achievements in US history. But Americans in the 1960s were far from united on the idea.

President John F. Kennedy spoke to Congress when he announced his goal to land a person on the moon.

The moon project was called Project Apollo. The National Aeronautics and Space Administration (NASA) had to figure out how to send people to the moon. That took a lot of time and money. Project Apollo cost approximately $25 billion. That would be equivalent to more than $150 billion in 2020. And that's not including the money spent on the earlier manned spaceflight programs, Mercury and Gemini. These programs laid the groundwork for Apollo.

Many Americans today would say the moon landing was worth it. But most Americans during the 1960s did not feel that way. They felt that the money should be spent on problems the United States was facing. Civil rights activist Ralph Abernathy led a protest at NASA. He said that there were Americans who did not have the money for basic needs. He said that if the United States could support Apollo, it could support its people.

Even some scientists did not approve. The money spent on Apollo meant there was less government

MOON
LANDINGS

Apollo 11 is the most famous moon landing mission. But NASA later made five more moon landings. This map shows where each mission landed. How does knowing that there were several moon landings help you understand the importance of the Apollo 11 mission?

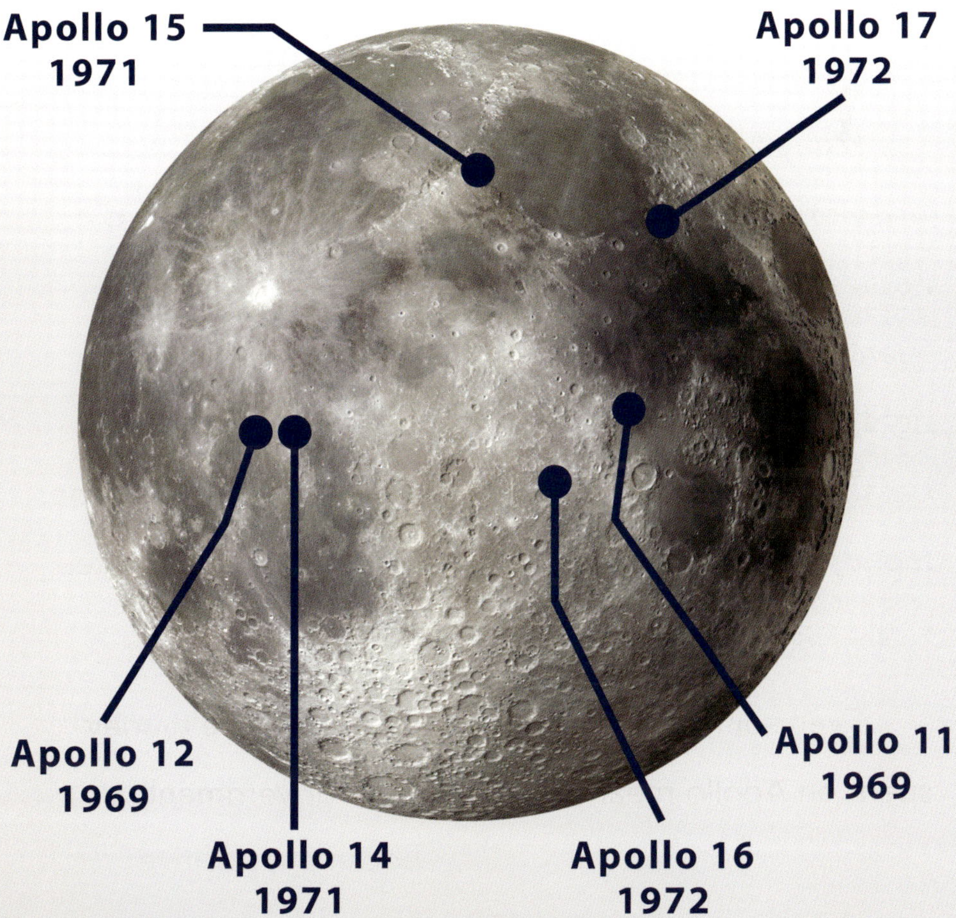

PERSPECTIVES

WHY GO TO THE MOON?

President Kennedy had many reasons for wanting to send Americans to the moon. One reason was to prove that the United States could do it. Kennedy gave a speech at Rice University in September 1962. In it he said:

> ***We choose to go to the moon. We choose to go to the moon in this decade . . . not because [it is] easy, but because [it is] hard, because that goal will serve to organize and measure the best of our energies and skills, because that challenge is one that we are willing to accept, one we are unwilling to postpone, and one which we intend to win.***

funding for studying Earth. They argued that studying Earth was more important to humanity. They also thought that it would be better to send up unmanned spacecraft, such as satellites. These would cost much less than human space exploration.

MOON MIX-UP

Despite these concerns, the moon landing was a major event. Criticisms of the program mostly faded over time. The landing became a positive

American memory. Millions of Americans watched the landing broadcast. Many remembered exactly where they were and what they were doing when Armstrong took the first steps on the moon.

They also remembered the first words he said. Those watching leaned toward their television sets. They heard Armstrong say, "That's one small step for man, one giant leap for mankind." But this is not what Armstrong remembered saying. He remembered saying, "That's one small step for *a* man." This statement meant that it was one small step for a person to take, but it was a huge leap forward in achievement for humanity. At least, that is what he meant to say. Later analysis showed that the word *a* may have been lost. This was because the communication system was not very good.

CONSPIRACY THEORIES

Landing on the moon was such a hard thing to do that some people do not believe it really happened. They think NASA faked it. Some people feel the United

States did this to score a victory over the Soviet Union. There are all sorts of conspiracy theories about the moon landing. But there is plenty of evidence to show these theories aren't true.

One of the most famous images of Apollo 11 is of the astronauts planting the US flag on the moon. People said this was fake because the flag looks like it is blowing in the wind, even though there is no wind on the moon. However, the flag is sticking out because it is held that

"HOUSTON . . ."

One of the most famous Apollo missions never made it to the moon. Apollo 13 launched on April 11, 1970. But a malfunction ended the moon mission and endangered the astronauts. Their story was told in the movie *Apollo 13*. Actor Tom Hanks played the mission's commander, James Lovell. One of the movie's most famous lines happens when an electrical problem causes an oxygen tank to explode. Hanks says, "Houston, we have a problem." But in real life, astronaut Jack Swigert first said, "I believe we've had a problem here." When asked to repeat, Lovell said, "Houston, we've had a problem."

The flag has ripples because the rod could not fully extend.

way by a metal rod. If there were no rod, the flag would drop straight down.

Other people said it was suspicious that photos from the moon show a black sky with no stars. But the photos were taken in daylight. Stars are not visible during the day on Earth, either. The moon was too bright for cameras to pick up the faint stars.

The cameras were also specially modified. The astronauts could not hold cameras while in their bulky suits. So NASA found another way for its astronauts to take pictures. There is a famous picture of Aldrin on the moon. Armstrong took the picture. He can be seen in the reflection of Aldrin's visor. People said Armstrong was not holding a camera in the reflection. So people thought the picture had to be fake. But Armstrong had the camera mounted to his suit. That is where the picture came from.

Despite all this evidence, some people still believe the moon landing was faked. But Armstrong and Aldrin didn't care. They knew what they had done. The proof is still on the moon with the equipment they left behind.

STRAIGHT TO THE SOURCE

The *Los Angeles Sentinel* was a newspaper. It was written and edited by Black people. In 1969, it published an opinion article by Booker Griffin. Griffin thought that Apollo cost too much money:

> *America's landing on the moon is one of the miracles of the ages. Few instances in the chronicles of man . . . were as significant. . . .*
>
> *Taken at face value, it would seem that all Americans would rejoice at such a monumental occurrence. I do not.*
>
> *The high priority that this country has put on landing on the moon and exploring outer space in the face of deplorable human suffering in this nation and throughout the world again asserts the fact that mechanical values supersede human values in this country.*

Source: Booker Griffin. "Moon Dust and Black Disgust." *Los Angeles Sentinel*, 24 July 1969, p. B7.

CHANGING MINDS

Do you think it was right for the United States to spend so much money on the Apollo missions? Imagine your friend has the opposite opinion. Write a short essay trying to change your friend's mind. Make sure you include facts and details to support your position.

CHAPTER THREE

ONLY WHITE MEN WORK FOR NASA?

The workforce of NASA in the 1950s and 1960s looked a lot like the typical businesses at the time. Almost all the employees were white men. All the astronauts were white men. So were all the people representing NASA. To the American public, it looked like white men were doing all the work. But that was far from the truth. There were many thousands of people behind the scenes.

Mary Jackson became NASA's first Black female engineer in 1958.

Most women who worked as computers at NACA had college degrees in math or other sciences.

COMPUTERS AND OTHER ROLES

In the days before computers, mathematical calculations were done by people. *Computer* was a job title. Human computers performed calculations, analyzed data, and more.

The computer program for spaceflight research started under the National Advisory Committee for Aeronautics (NACA). NACA was formed in 1915. It was an organization segregated by race. The Black employees were not allowed to mix with their white coworkers.

HISTORY MAKERS LOST

One of the worst disasters in NASA history occurred on January 28, 1986. The space shuttle *Challenger* broke apart shortly after launch. All seven crew members were killed. Some of them were NASA history makers. The shuttle carried teacher Christa McAuliffe. She had won a national contest to become the first teacher in space. Also on board was Ellison S. Onizuka. Onizuka had been the first Asian American in space on his previous flight. And Judith Resnik had become the first Jewish woman in space in 1984.

In 1958 a new agency was created. This was NASA. NASA was built around NACA. It was never segregated. But NASA's hiring practices were not always fair. It often did not consider women and Black people for advanced roles. Black men typically worked in manual labor or in service positions. Women were hired as computers. However, not all employees were treated as equals.

HIDDEN FIGURES

NASA could not have functioned without human computers. Their math skills helped chart the course for NASA's rockets. But for many years, computers never got the credit they deserved. Their names were sometimes left off NASA's reports.

In 2016, a book came out called *Hidden Figures*. This book finally put the contributions of the computers in the spotlight. A movie version came out in the same year. The book focused on Dorothy Vaughan, Mary Jackson, Christine Darden, and Katherine Johnson. Vaughan started working as a computer in the 1940s. Jackson and Johnson were hired in the 1950s.

Christine Darden started as a computer at NASA and became an engineer in 1973.

The women worked at the segregated NACA until NASA was created in 1958.

All three women made big contributions to NASA. Jackson did experiments using wind tunnels to study aerodynamics. Vaughan helped program NASA's electronic computers. And Johnson helped chart the path for Apollo to get to the moon. These women are just a few of the lesser-known contributors to the space program.

PERSPECTIVES

DOROTHY VAUGHAN

Dorothy Vaughan was a high school math teacher. Then she went to work for NACA in 1943. Vaughan led the all-Black team of computers at NACA for years. She was the first Black supervisor in NACA history. Computers like Vaughan worked hard to do their jobs despite the unequal treatment. "I changed what I could, and what I couldn't, I endured," Vaughan said. She retired in 1971. By that time, her team had become part of NASA.

Many of the computers did not live to see their story told. Both Jackson and

Katherine Johnson had a 33-year career at NACA and later NASA.

Vaughan had passed away by the time the book was released. In 2015, President Barack Obama awarded Johnson the Presidential Medal of Freedom. That is the highest honor a civilian can receive.

CHAPTER FOUR

NASA INVENTIONS

People have attributed many inventions that they saw used in space to NASA. For example, Velcro played a big role in the space program. The hook and loop fasteners helped hold objects down in microgravity. But NASA did not invent the technology. It was invented in the 1940s in Switzerland.

NASA thought the technology would be great for spaceflight. It worked closely with the Velcro company to put Velcro on suits, spacecraft, and more. NASA said

Astronaut Neil Armstrong, *front*, used Velcro to secure his wristwatch around his space suit.

later that astronauts could not have worked in space without Velcro.

NASA research has led to the invention of many household products. But NASA can't claim credit for all of them. Some products it merely used and did not invent.

TANG

Tang is an orange-flavored powdered drink mix that became popular in the 1960s. It became popular because it was used in space. Tang seemed like a product specially made for space. It was lightweight and did not go bad. Plus, it was easy for astronauts to make. But NASA did not invent the drink.

Instead, NASA helped promote it. The drink was released in 1959. It did not sell well. However, NASA thought it was a perfect drink for astronauts. Tang was on board with John Glenn when he became the first US astronaut to orbit Earth in 1962.

By 1965, the company that made Tang was using NASA in its ads. People wanted to drink what astronauts drank. Tang became a success.

TEFLON

Many home cooks appreciate the Teflon coating on their pans. This material keeps food from sticking to hot surfaces. People may want to thank NASA for that. NASA did use the material. But NASA didn't invent this either.

Teflon was invented by the DuPont company in 1938. Many years later, NASA

ASTRONAUT ICE CREAM

Visitors to space museum gift shops have their pick of many souvenirs. One popular item is freeze-dried ice cream. This product is sold as the kind that astronauts eat. Ice cream like that was tested in 1968. But it was never used in space. The freeze-dried stuff crumbles a lot. That is not good for sensitive spacecraft instruments. Real ice cream is actually pretty easy to take to space. It sticks together in microgravity. If it melts, it doesn't drip. Astronauts today enjoy ice cream regularly.

needed a material that could stand up to heat. It decided to use Teflon on space suits, heat shields, and more.

PERSPECTIVES

HONORING ROBERT GODDARD

Robert H. Goddard was an engineer and professor. He experimented with rockets. Goddard invented the liquid-fueled rocket. This technology made modern rockets possible. Goddard died in 1945, before NASA even existed. But NASA's first spaceflight center was named in his honor. Goddard once said, "It is difficult to say what is impossible, for the dream of yesterday is the hope of today and the reality of tomorrow."

NASA'S ACTUAL INVENTIONS

There are many products and technologies that NASA has invented. Its engineers work to advance science and technology.

NASA helped make computers smaller. Computers used to be huge. NASA's spacecraft needed lightweight computers to fly. Project Apollo pioneered the use of small yet powerful computers.

NASA began a program in 1994 to develop a new remote-controlled aircraft. It required solar power. In order to fly, the solar panels had to be very lightweight and powerful. Home solar panels today use this technology.

These are just a few examples. Even when NASA did not invent things, it often helped make them more common or cheaper. NASA is about more than just spaceflight. It is a massive research and development organization.

EXPLORE ONLINE

Chapter Four discusses some of the things NASA did and did not invent. Read the list of inventions at the following website. As you know, every source is different. What information does the website give about NASA's inventions? How is the information from the website the same as the information in Chapter Four? What new information did you learn from the website?

20 INVENTIONS WE WOULDN'T HAVE WITHOUT SPACE TRAVEL

abdocorelibrary.com/fact-fiction-space-age

NASA

CHAPTER FIVE

NASA DOES WHAT?

NASA's mission is pretty clear. It seeks to advance science and technology to improve life on Earth. But even with that noble mission, some people still suspect that NASA is up to no good.

There have been many wild theories about NASA. Some include NASA's involvement with aliens. Interest in aliens started before NASA was created. Once the United States began exploring space, some people believed that NASA must be connected with aliens.

Kennedy Space Center is one of NASA's ten major centers for research, development, and missions.

THE BLACK KNIGHT

One of the most famous conspiracy theories involving NASA took off in 1998. That was when scientists began building the International Space Station (ISS) in space. The ISS is a spacecraft in permanent orbit around Earth. Astronauts live and do experiments in the ISS. Mission STS-88 was the first space shuttle mission to the ISS. During this 1998 mission, astronauts took several pictures. Some of those pictures showed a strange black object floating in space.

For years, some people had believed in the existence of the Black Knight. The Black Knight was supposedly an alien satellite observing Earth. To these people, the 1998 photos confirmed that the Black Knight existed.

But the photos are easily explained. The object was just a piece of debris that came loose as astronauts built the ISS. Former NASA space engineer James Oberg went to great lengths to prove this. He had worked on

A blanket was the piece of debris that people believed was the Black Knight satellite.

the mission. He also knew the person who had taken the pictures. He explained away the theories. The debris was definitely not an alien satellite.

SETI

People have long believed that NASA knows about aliens. Some even believe that it has been in contact with aliens. In reality, NASA used to fund a program called the Search for Extraterrestrial Intelligence (SETI). The program started in 1985. Scientists in the program listened for possible alien signals from outer space. But there was no contact with aliens. In 1993, the program was canceled.

The search carries on with the SETI Institute. The institute is separate from NASA, but it took the SETI name. It uses radio telescopes to scan the skies. These telescopes are very powerful. They can detect radio waves coming from the deepest parts of space. SETI has heard signals over the years.

PERSPECTIVES
JAMES OBERG

James Oberg learned that people had made a conspiracy theory out of a piece of space debris. So he shared the truth. Oberg said, "They are probably some of the weirdest-looking 70 mm photos to ever come out of the space shuttle program. And apparently a NASA website update made the original links inoperative, sparking concerns over a cover-up. All normal journalistic practices—determining the timeline, asking witnesses, searching for the wider context—were skipped."

But many natural objects in space give off radio waves. No one has found any evidence of alien life.

THE SETI INSTITUTE

The SETI Institute's research covers many branches of science, including astronomy and biology. Its scientists study not only the depths of space but also life on Earth. The institute seeks to answer three questions. How does life develop? Where else in the universe does it exist? And how can we find it?

NOT LIKE THE MOVIES

Space stations and radio telescopes may seem like science fiction. But NASA's work doesn't look like what people see in movies and on television. One example is in the 1980 film *The Empire Strikes Back*. In one scene, Han Solo steers his ship through an asteroid field. The huge asteroids threaten to beat the spacecraft to a pulp.

But in real life, asteroids pose little threat to spacecraft. NASA would know. It has sent several missions through the asteroid belt between Mars

NASA'S BUDGET

NASA's budget for 2020 was just over $21 billion. This chart shows how NASA divided that money. What do you think this chart says about what NASA's priorities are?

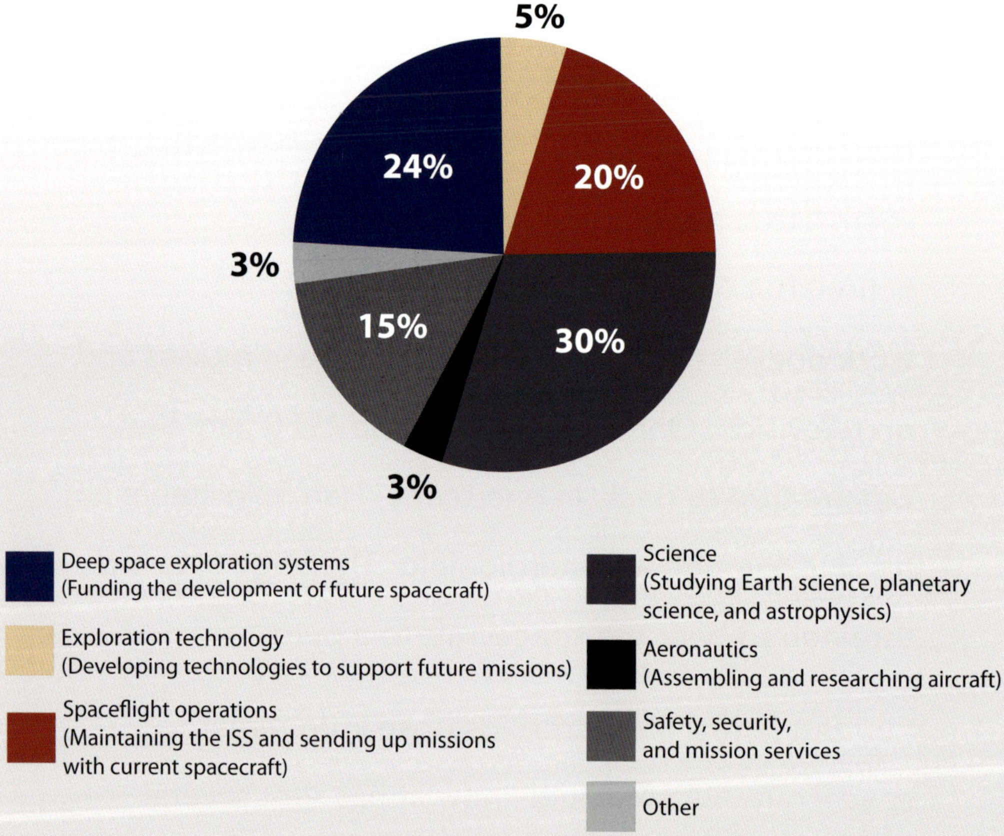

Source: *Explore Budget Estimates Briefing Book: FY 2020.* NASA, 2020, p. 10.

and Jupiter. That is where most of the solar system's asteroids are located. But space is huge. Even in the asteroid belt, the odds of hitting an asteroid are really small. As of 2020, no spacecraft has accidentally hit one.

Members of the public may not always understand what NASA does. But NASA has achieved a lot in space exploration and other areas of science. The space age has resulted in great achievements that have impacted the lives of people around the world.

FURTHER EVIDENCE

Chapter Five talks about NASA's mission. What was one of the main points of this chapter? What evidence is included to support this point? Review the website below. Does it add any new evidence?

OUR MISSION AND VALUES

abdocorelibrary.com/fact-fiction-space-age

IMPORTANT DATES

1957
On October 4, the Soviet Union successfully launches *Sputnik 1*, starting the space age.

1958
The National Aeronautics and Space Administration (NASA) is created. NASA's workers are not segregated.

1961
On May 25, President John F. Kennedy gives a speech to announce a project with the goal of landing men on the moon. But the American people are divided on whether such a trip is worth it.

1962
Astronaut John Glenn brings Tang on his mission to orbit Earth. While NASA had not invented the drink, NASA does promote it by having it on board the spacecraft.

1969
On July 20, Apollo 11 lands on the moon. Humans step onto the moon for the first time.

1998
Photos of a mysterious object add to theories about an alien spacecraft floating around Earth. But this object is easily proven to be a piece of debris from the International Space Station.

2015
Former NASA computer Katherine Johnson receives the Presidential Medal of Freedom. Johnson's contributions to the space program had not been previously well known.

STOP AND THINK

Tell the Tale

Chapter One of this book describes the American reaction to the Soviet Union launching *Sputnik 1*. Imagine you are an American citizen in 1957. Write 200 words about what it would be like to learn about *Sputnik 1*. How would you feel when you learned this news?

Surprise Me

Chapter Four discusses inventions by NASA. After reading this book, what two or three facts about NASA's inventions did you find most surprising? Write a few sentences about each fact. Why did you find each fact surprising?

Dig Deeper

After reading this book, what questions do you still have about the space age? With an adult's help, find a few reliable sources to help you answer your questions. Write a paragraph about what you learned.

Say What?

Studying space exploration can mean learning a lot of new vocabulary. Find five words in this book you have never heard before. Use a dictionary to find out what they mean. Then write each meaning in your own words and use each word in a new sentence.

GLOSSARY

aerodynamics
the study of how air flows around moving objects

conspiracy theory
a belief that an event is the result of a secret plot

debris
a piece of something that has been destroyed

extraterrestrial
coming from somewhere other than Earth

heat shield
a surface that protects spacecraft from too much heat

microgravity
the condition in which people and things seem weightless

orbit
the path of something around another object

satellite
an object or vehicle that orbits a more massive object in space

segregate
to separate based on race

space shuttle
a reusable spacecraft that transports people and cargo

ONLINE RESOURCES

To learn more about the facts and fiction of the space age, visit our free resource websites below.

Core Library CONNECTION
FREE! COMMON CORE MULTIMEDIA RESOURCES

Visit **abdocorelibrary.com** or scan this QR code for free Common Core resources for teachers and students, including vetted activities, multimedia, and booklinks, for deeper subject comprehension.

Booklinks NONFICTION NETWORK
FREE! ONLINE NONFICTION RESOURCES

Visit **abdobooklinks.com** or scan this QR code for free additional online weblinks for further learning. These links are routinely monitored and updated to provide the most current information available.

LEARN MORE

Borgert-Spaniol, Megan. *Katherine Johnson: Guiding Spacecraft.* Abdo Publishing, 2018.

Doudna, Kelly. *Space Exploration.* Abdo Publishing, 2017.

INDEX

About the Author

Douglas Hustad is a freelance author of primarily science and history books for young people. He, his wife, and their two dogs live in the northern suburbs of San Diego, California.